TESTIMONY

TESTIMONY

Poems by

Anita Barrows

Cover design by Shay Culligan
Cover photograph by Nora Barrows-Friedman

ISBN: 978-1-954353-28-2

Kelsay Books
502 South 1040 East, A-119
American Fork, Utah, 84003

for my children and grandchildren
for Joanna Macy

and in memory of George Oppen

...We have chosen the meaning
Of being numerous....

Acknowledgments

Portions of these poems have been read on the BBC's Third Programme and have been presented by The Naropa Institute.

In the dark times coming
Will there be singing?
Yes, there will be singing
About the dark times

—Bertolt Brecht

Dadme las luchas
de cada dia
porque ellas
son mi canto

—Pablo Neruda

Let everything happen to you: beauty and terror.

—Rainer Maria Rilke

#1

Berkeley, California

I dream I'm driving to the house of a friend
who, in the dream, is dying. The road
I'm driving passes through
deep woods. Ferns. Equisetum.
A stream so swollen with rainfall
I can hear it from the car.
My friend in the dream is dying
because his lungs cannot use the air.
His lungs are filled
with cancer instead of oxygen. I think,
as I drive, of trees
breathing. The road
winds higher into the hills.
I think of cells
closing down, each by each.

.

Like the metal shade
a shop owner pulls down
at the end of each day
over the window of his
shop, the bright display.
Inside, all the wares.
His life. His livelihood. Dishes
lined up, one after the next. Enameled pots
of various sizes, some made
for soup, some for boiled eggs.

11

．

When I arrive, people are lined
in front of his house. I wonder if my friend
has already died, but no,
they are permitted to enter his room
through a wide blue doorway, then another doorway.
He tells each one there is nothing he needs. Nothing.

．

When Rosamund was dying her bed faced the mountains
called *Sangre de Cristo,* Blood of Christ.
Each day she would wake and track the sun
as it moved across the vast
sky: first behind her, where
she couldn't see it, though she knew it had risen
from the shadow her house cast on the field
between her and the mountains. Then it would light
her rug, then her bed. Then at last it would come
to rest behind the mountains, and the blood
of Christ every evening flooded the world.

．

Two mourning doves in the Monterey Pine.
The pineapple guava tree cut down
that stood twenty-eight years
at the window. Where
will the towhees go, the cedar waxwings? Once Ciel,
seven or eight, sat at the kitchen table drawing a dove
who came to eat at the feeder. Black

sunflower seeds spilled and spilled
into the garden. It was summer, she
was spending whole days at my house. The dove
ate. Ciel drew slowly, carefully,
in pencil, then wrote
at the bottom of the page, *"The most*
beautiful dove and the longest-staying."

.

What stays? The sea, its relentless rhythms?
Fish are dying, reefs disappearing.
Why would one bird stay long enough
for a child to draw it, then fly off
into the fog that, already, was coming in
from the Pacific? A man sits in his bed in a dream,
needing nothing. Refusing this or that.
No reassurance. No fragment of memory. No food.
Not a book not a song not a word not even a touch.

.

I stand in line
in the dream, wondering
if I have anything new to offer, anything
of value. For months it has been difficult for me
to write poetry. I think, sometimes,
that it would be better to stop, be still, to try
to content myself with listening. The stream
persists over the sound of my car's
engine. The sun sets behind the blood of Christ
and someone else watches it from the same
room. Who was it who said

nothing you do will make a difference
yet it remains essential that you do it?

.

I have the drawing in a folder. The dove
that was the most beautiful and the longest-staying
sits forever on the wooden plank
of my feeder, head
down, though you can see one eye
that seems to look at Ciel
through the window
she also drew. A few black
sunflower seeds fall
through the blank air
to the invisible ground beneath.

#2

North Fork of the Yuba River
California

The river more full this summer
than last, the snows still melting
in July, still pouring down
from seven thousand, eight thousand feet
over the rocks, into the crevices
between boulders, pooling deep, cold,
nearly still enough to swim in
at the place I have walked to
each year each day I am here
each summer—half the summers of my life—
over the stones that remain the same
and the stones changed by this river
slowly subtly unremarkably

.

A child I knew, daughter
of a family I know well,
drowned in the Pacific a week ago,
pulled out by a rogue wave.
How can I speak of this
alongside anything else?
Her small hands
The white sundress she wore
And how she might have sung
that morning, walking
the stony trail along the shoreline

.

(morning texts)

The mother of a child
who was a classmate
of the drowned girl
writes me, *What shall I tell my son?*
Another sends me a photograph
from a trail in Colorado
This is the place I love best on this earth, she writes
And I, this morning, stand here
in the shadows of mountains
on a dirt road
in the place I love best on this earth
beside the North Fork of the Yuba River,
five thousand feet above sea level
Millions of feet below the constellations
that are hidden by day by
light by brilliant
light

.

I had not thought I would write
about the girl who drowned.
I do not want to make of her death
any history of my own.
There are some things, I write
to the mother of her friend,
that cannot be spoken in any way
but the stark, bare truth

16

The child the wave the disappearance
into the sea and the not
coming back onto land alive.
The rescue workers bent over her body.
Pounding her chest, frantically breathing air
into her mouth. The child
unresponsive, her lungs unable
by then to make any use anymore
of the oxygen of this world.

.

Morning lengthens. The child's sister
sobs in her mother's arms, *"She never even
got to learn long division."*
How many times does one life
go into another? Five? Ten? A dozen?
The number of months between birth
and being swallowed by the Pacific? The number
of fingers, toes, eyes, knees, ears? The number
of heartbeats? And what, if
anything, is the remainder?

.

I sit here
surrounded by cedar, lodgepole pine, Jeffrey pine,
on a Monday morning at the end of July
in the summer of my seventieth year.
Sunlight falls from the east, illumines the tips
of pine needles; turns, in the mild
breeze, the undersides of leaves
to quivering silver.

I have come to this place every summer
for half my life. I have come
with my daughters when they were small
and when they were older; with Ciel, my granddaughter;
with generations of dogs—lively, exuberant,
racing to hurl themselves into the river.
I have come here with the dearest
among my friends: long
conversations into the night as the world
burns, as stars burn and burn their way
to us through the aeons. Always I have come
with my hands empty. Always I have come
asking *why* and *how* and *how*
much longer and *to*
what end?

.

From the city my friends and my neighbors
write to me. Their grief and their discoveries
appear on the little screen of my phone
when I walk out to where
there's reception, morning and evening,
half a mile up the road
that winds higher into the mountains.
One sends me a poem. One
sends me a photograph of her dog.
Several, this morning, write of the child
who drowned. *Is it wrong,* one
asks, *to say that her death makes the deaths*
of all of our children seem closer,
more possible? Another writes
of the refugees, the children
among them drowning on

18

faulty boats, suffocating
on boats packed impossibly tight:
Is it wrong, she asks,
to compare the death of this child
to these?

.

She was the one
we knew, I think
as I walk through shadows
of tall trees. The one whose death
makes each of these deaths
particular, individual, riveting.

.

We know, we cannot keep
from knowing, that the earth is imperiled.
Yet the beauty of this place
sears me to my core.
I am a hewn log, a husk of cicada,
a stone split open for light to enter.
Thousands of suns flaming
in thousands of leaves.

#3

North fork of the Yuba River
California

Saw two boys—sixteen? seventeen?—
with a small dog, some kind
of terrier mix, go down
to the mountain pool. Cold river, mid-summer,
the swimming hole deep and green, stillness
between turbulences, the river moving, moving.
Saw, from a trail on the opposite bank, the dog
jump into the water, swim around and around,
skirting the place where it opened
into the downrushing river, the two boys
now with their backs to him, drinking
whatever it was
they had brought to drink. The dog
circling and circling, elated
at first, then desperate, his short legs
tiring. Trying to pull himself up
onto land and unable, the sides of the swimming hole
too steep, too sheer. So cold, the river
issuing from the mountains. The boys
unaware, the dog
swimming more slowly now, tired,
desperation giving way to fatigue,
to a kind of resigned hopeless occasional pawing
at the gravelly edges, the kids
still drinking and laughing and I
helpless, too far away, the bank
too steep for me to descend, my voice
calling to them from the opposite side
of the river inaudible
over the rush and pooling of water.

.

I am thinking of Hammed, age seven, 2008,
whose house in Gaza City was bombed, seventeen members
of his family killed. Grandparents.
His mother. His infant sister.
(Dadme las luchas de cada dia) Hammed,
sitting on the floor
of the hospital playroom with his one as yet
unmanageable prosthetic leg and one
of the legs he was born with, pushing (with the hands
he still had) a small blue metal toy ambulance
across the floor. Whirr of the wheels, the little
battery-powered light on the roof,
above where the driver would be *(porque
ellas son mi canto)* blinking and blinking and blinking.

.

Was the dog saved? Did one of the boys
turn around at last, dive into the water,
grasp him with his strong teenage arms, push him up
into the strong teenage arms of the other? In the end
I had to walk on. I had somewhere
to go, someone waiting for me. My voice,
my witnessing, my frantic waving,
useless.

.

I want to believe
the dog survived. I want to believe
there was really nothing
I could do. I want to believe
that, rescued, he shook off
the icy water, lay down
on the stones and browning
pineneedles, closed his eyes
under the afternoon sun
and slept, listening to the kids
resuming their talk.
Walked back with them later
up the reedy bank as though nothing
of this had happened.

.

The way a single tree
at a particular hour
in a particular region
of the western Sierra
at a particular
time of the year
catches the light. That is
nearly gone now
even as I write, the sun
moving lower
across the sky, air
ringing with heat though we've come
to the end of summer.

#4

Syria
Pacific coast

A child in a war-ravaged city
learns to swim from her father.
This while bombs
fall on her country. Every day before dawn
she makes her way, holding
her father's hand,
to the municipal pool
a few blocks from her apartment.
Here in the still
turquoise depth, arms
and legs rhythmically
moving. Outside,
in the city, buildings
reduced to rebar.
The sounds of bombing
dulled by water.

.

Her father knows stories
of those who have had to leap
from boats packed with people
fleeing, swim to a shore they can barely see
from such a distance. He is telling his child
to make small adjustments
to the rhythm of her breathing, the angle
at which she must lift her arms
out of the water. Standing there
on the edge of the pool, he thinks
What I am teaching her may one day
save her. Or it may not.

.

I want to tell you now
about starfish. Thousands of them
found dead on Pacific beaches, the ocean
changed: too warm. Five-pointed bodies
disintegrating from the inside: Starfish
Wasting Disease: their skeletons
destroyed. From cliffs
above the sand you could see
them: thousands of stars
washed up, inert.

.

As though the sky itself were emptied.
Stars poured out onto the sand. No longer
bright. No longer flickering.

.

It's quiet here. The pool becomes shelter, home.
Movement, resistance to movement. The child knows
she will soon need to climb
out of the water.
Shower. Dress for school.
Her father stands on the pool's
edge, blue towel in his hands. Tenderly
he wraps it around his
child. Notes how thin
she is, though her stroke today
was strong. *Improving,*
he thinks, and stops
his next thought: *For what?*

To walk home,
he thinks,
will not be, will not
ever again be
to return to everything as it was:
A breakfast of bread, cheese, boiled eggs
on the table. Laughter,
conversation. Music
on the radio, a song you dance to.

.

Let the water carry your weight: when
Nora, my first child
was still in my womb,
I swam every day
in the university pool in the hills.
She turned in me as I lifted
my face from the water, wind
coming in from the ocean, moving
the oaks, the eucalyptus. So many years
ago and still I remember
the way that heaviness left me
when I stepped into the water, stretched
my arms, let myself be held.

.

A father walks home
from the pool,
holding his daughter's hand,
choosing back streets,

not telling her why. The child
knowing not to ask. They quicken their pace,
arrive, this time, safely. The father
turns on the radio, the child
goes to her room, gathers
her books, her papers, for school.
This could be a story
happening anywhere
but it's happening here,
gunfire outside, news
of who's missing

.

Suddenly people begin
finding starfish. Starfish
beginning to line the beaches,
healthy, thriving.
Beach after beach, all the way
up the coast. Someone takes a group of them
to a laboratory, samples their DNA.
It seems they have made
a spontaneous mutation.
It seems they are finding a way to persist.

.

What you know about water
and the heaviness of water, about your body
and its weight, about the fear
of what you may see
when you rise above the surface

—may help you
or it may not. A city
bombed to ruins has one
building on a block of ruins
still spared, which happens to be
the municipal pool. The sky
turning pearl-gray as day
unfolds. Din of planes
whistling toward their targets
mingles with sounds of morning
from open
windows: dishes clattering. Voices.
Barking dogs.

.

Child, somersaulting
as you turn, your head
never wholly rising
above the surface, your father
coaching you
from the pool's edge,
can you trust the strength
of your arms, the speed
of your legs? Can you believe
what you know
will outlast the wreckage?

27

#5

Berkeley, California
Mostar, Bosnia

What solace is there oh my friends what solace
Warm September sunlight, ripened sunlight
Sunlight through branches of persimmon,
dry leaves on the grass. What
solace for the mother
whose child will not awaken again
We can't know We won't know
When the plane flying over the city

.

will choose our house
as its target

.

Ivana telling me about Sarajevo,
how night after night
her family sat in the single room that had
no windows. *I don't know which was worse,* she
says, *the fear of being bombed*
or the boredom
of having to sit there with the lights off the radio
off my grandmother with her insufferable
asthmatic breathing. What solace *My sorrow*
Rexroth writing in Kings' Canyon
after his wife's death, *My sorrow*
is so wide I cannot see across it

28

·

George gone. Denise gone. Rukeyser. Adrienne.
Ginsberg whose broken leg—
London, '73—gave me the chance
to drive him around in my small
two-seater. An insect—ant or gnat—
on Hampstead Heath one spring afternoon
crawling onto a page
of the book he was reading: he gently
brushed it away, back into
the grass, so carefully. Later wrote,
Fly away, tiny mite, even your life
is tender These were
my teachers, those whose words infused
my words, whose intentions in poetry
shaped mine. Whose manner
of seeing.

·

That summer at the camp
for the children from Sarajevo, most of them
orphaned by the wars, some,
like Ivana, who had also lost siblings
and whose grandmother was too sick
to care for her. Viva, my child,
seventeen at the time,
taking all the money I'd given her
to spend with her friends at the snack bar
where they danced to European rock
through the long, warm nights—

taking the ferry to Korchula on her day off
from being a counselor,
spending all that money on clothes,
bathing suits, for two little girls
who had come for the month of camp
with one plastic baggie between them: a couple of pairs
of underwear, one sweater to share.

.

At sixteen, cutting school
to take the Long Island Railroad
into the city
to see Rukeyser read at NYU.
I walked til I found
the large, windowed room,
found every seat taken. Hesitated
at the doorway, thinking
I should leave, taking it as a sign
I did not
belong. What was it
the moment before I turned to go
that made Rukeyser look
my way, see me
stopped, standing outside the door,
then nod her head at
me, gesture
for me to come in? And when
I crossed the threshold and stood just
inches inside, leaning
against the wall of that room, she
gestured to me again, this time

to sit by her feet on the
carpeted floor, and did not
begin reading (her strong her
courageous) poems
until I was there.

.

All my life remembering that moment.
Being welcomed. Being asked inside.
Made room for.

.

One hand holding Ivana's head.
My other hand at her waist.
She is floating in the water.
She who has been afraid of water
is letting me hold her, letting the warm
almost waveless, lakelike Adriatic
hold her. Ivana,
who had been walking in Sarajevo
behind her brother, lagging
(to his annoyance) behind, looking
(she tells me) at her
own image (a girl, slender,
thirteen) in a storefront window
when she heard the explosion.
Saw her brother lying on the sidewalk.
Face down. Not crying
out. A pool of his blood

and still she didn't
understand what
had happened. A crowd
gathering now around him, women,
police, Ivana
pushing past them, screaming
her brother's name over
and over. I am
holding her now
in the Adriatic,
shallow enough, close enough
to the shore so I
can stand, assuring her
that the water
will stay calm, there's no
reason to fear, promising
her I won't
let her go.

.

I write
for you now, friends, teachers, I
coming to the end of summer
in my seventieth year,
my three dogs sleeping
in mottled shadows of trees, my
children not far, my grandchildren.
Can I preserve at least this image? This day?
Leaves browning at the edges
in afternoon heat but still
on the branch.
Fruit not yet ready.

#6

Berkeley, California

Once when Ciel was on the highest bar
of the climbing structure
in the park overlooking the freeway
and I behind her
we saw a brown dog
on the divider strip, frantically looking
for a way back to one side or the other. Everywhere
cars going seventy, eighty,
no space between them
to make it through.
The unbearable wait and then
the more unbearable instant
when the dog
leapt out between cars, wove his way
as the traffic, incredibly, slowed, stopped, and he
made it across to the side our park was on,
racing through weeds
alongside the access road
as though it hadn't just nearly cost him his life.

.

Viva knew a boy who shot someone by accident,
killed him, then ran, thinking he could hide.
He wasn't a friend, just someone Viva
went to school with, a kid who'd sat at the back
of Chemistry. She saw his name
in the paper after some other kid
who'd witnessed the shooting
told the cops what happened: the frantic running, the gun
tossed in a dumpster.

Viva said he was shy, skinny, never talked,
always handed in his homework. A neighbor
came up with bail
when the kid was found, three weeks later,
living in an abandoned car. His dad
too far gone with alcohol to care
what happened, no mom
on the scene for years.

.

I am trying to write a poem about redemption.
I am trying to show you
the skill, the resilience
of the dog, the quick reflexes of the drivers,
the desperate concern of a five year old child
looking down from a climbing structure
at a dog trying to save his own life.
I am trying to say that, in the absence
of father, mother, there may be someone
willing to take out an equity line of credit
on his already over-mortgaged house
to post bail for a kid who grew up
next door. I am trying to think
what it must have been like for the kid
hiding out in a rusted car, eating
from trash cans,
contacting no one. Chilled. Scared.
My granddaughter
at five, crying about the dog
on the divider strip,
clutching my hand.

.

And isn't that
what we do? Some days
maybe more than others: Stare straight
into the darkness
and hold on with one hand
to whatever might keep us
from falling?

#7

Prison, USA
Bethlehem
Hewlett, New York
Berkeley, California

What solace oh my friends what
solace. People in cages, meals
thrown at them through slots
in the metal doors, sometimes cold, sometimes
moldy, a hole in the floor
for pee shit vomit; who ever
cleans it? And they have to eat
and sleep in that same cell.

.

Nora saw a child and her father
crossing a checkpoint. The child was wearing a new
pink belt, and when the soldier
pointing his gun at her
told her to remove
the belt and hand it to him, she
cried. Refused. New pink shiny
plastic belt, like patent leather but
not, clearly new because when the father
knelt down in front of his child
and pleaded with her, tears
running down his cheeks,
and the child kept refusing
and crying, crying
and refusing, her father
begging her, gently
stroking her cheek (the gun
still pointed)—when at last

she gave in and took
the belt off there was no
crease yet in the belt where if
the child had had it even
a matter of weeks the buckle
would have worn a light
groove in the stiff pink plastic.

.

An old woman in line
behind them, trying to comfort
child, the father. The soldier
fingering the belt now
as though it were
filth, throwing it back
at the child, hurrying them
through the checkpoint, no
time even to slip the belt back
through the cotton loops of her jeans.
A child holding a pink
plastic belt, buckle
scraping the ground. Sadly,
as though suddenly it had lost
its meaning. Her father behind her, walking
head down, watching the silver metal
buckle drag through the dust.
A testimony of senselessness.
Nora, my daughter, my grown
child, watching. Documenting.

.

When I was ten I hauled some boards
on a rope up to a crook
between the top branches
of an elm; for months
climbed the rope, afternoons
after school: an apple, a book,
an empty lot near where I lived.
Then one Thursday came home
to the truck the men the buzz of the saw:
my boards strewn
on the ground, the perfectly angled branches
gone. I ran screaming
across the weedy lot
raging against the men
who went on sawing. Too loud
the sound of the chainsaw; not even a word
to me, skinny inaudible girl
in my green plaid skirt
thinking the single the last
act of love I could perform
for the tree I had failed
to save was to stand
and witness its dismemberment.

.

I stood til they drove away.
(Am I writing a litany of failure?)

Late October, the light
nearly bronze, oak leaves and sycamore
mulch in the gardens, a smell
of everything that is going to die
and be pressed by rain
into memory,
into the earth.

.

A spider is weaving her web
outside my window; filaments
catching the light. The wings
of some large insect she has caught,
half-consumed, transparent, laid
over the transparent web,
sear my heart with their beauty.
Do I cast my lot now
with this spider, not attempting
to do anything exceptional, making
from air and dust and the elements
of her body some durable
gesture of survival?

#8

Berkeley, California
Rikers Island, New York, New York
Oakland, California

I see their faces, They haunt me in the day. They come to me in the dark.
They force me to remember and they make me choose sides.

—Chris Hedges, 2015

A boy, sixteen, is jailed
for stealing a backpack he denies
he stole. He's beaten, starved,
locked in solitary. Three
and a half years.
He appeals his case. Pleads to be seen
by anyone who can help him. Minister?
Psychiatrist? At last
he's released, starts
college, only
to hang himself. In the hour
he dies, I am walking
the hills above this city, looking down
over freeways, boulevards
teeming with people,
the wild Pacific, fog
moving in from the west. I do not know
he is there, a continent away, seeing no farther
than the walls that caged him, caged
him even after
he was freed. *Freed?* Too far gone
into despair to think
of his mother, his brothers, a friend
who shot baskets with him on a schoolyard,
the sky he will never see again. A boy.
Forgive me. Forgive each one of us
our distance. Our uncaring. Our turning away.

.

Let me tell you: there are moments
I have no words
for this, not a cry, not even a syllable
of a lament. For whom
is this story supposed to be told?
For whom am I telling it?

.

A man I know went to the funeral
of a kid he read about in the paper
who was killed by police. He'd never seen
the kid, never been to the church
where the article said the funeral
would be; but on the morning
he'd read it would happen, he found himself
walking in, finding a seat
in a rear pew—as it
happened, next to a cousin
of the murdered kid. The cousin wept
when the minister spoke of the boy
just nineteen, working days
at a convenience store,
taking classes at night. My friend
left the funeral as he'd
come, alone. Went to his car. Drove home,
unable to stop seeing the face
of the boy,
also alone, skinny
dressed-up kid in his blue
satin-lined coffin.

.

When I write
of the savaged tree, the prisoner, the dog,
the child standing beside her father
at the checkpoint, I am
choosing sides.
I am casting my lot
with those whose work it is
to make a record,
to document grief. Empty hours. The roar
of bullhorns, the shadows of tanks.

.

What is it we belong to?
And what right do we have
to name our loneliness
kin to any other loneliness? Should ignorance
be forgiven? And by whom? *(Forgive them
for they know not
what they do…)* You
with your three dogs, your hiking shoes,
your gray hooded sweatshirt keeping you warm:
of whom do you ask
forgiveness? You whose car
is waiting for you
in the gravel parking lot at the end of the trail.
You whose children and grandchildren wake in their beds.

.

The threads stretch wider. What secures them?
Berkeley. Riker's Island. Brooklyn. The Bronx.
Life moves away from us and away.
Away and away
the days go, like leaves
of the gingkos
blown suddenly by a wind
as I waited yesterday afternoon
in traffic. Leaves.
Yellow and golden. Hundreds
of them falling
on asphalt, sidewalk, cars.
Leaves! And an old man,
bent, his cane propped beside him,
sitting on the bench
in front of the pie shop,
stretching wide his arms,
lifting his face,
unclenching his hands
to receive
whichever of them
might choose him.

#9

Berkeley, California
The Middle East

How we are saved
and lost and saved again. I told
a story to my granddaughter
when she was small
and afraid of water
about a water horse
who carries a girl like
Ciel on his back
out into the ocean. Slowly, hoof
after hoof, under the surface,
to its deepest depths.
It's raining again,
more rain than we can collect, flowing
in rivulets down steep streets. Lost
to us, unusable. So much
has been lost to us. The rain
heavier now, running along
the veins of leaves. Bending them, bowing
them. Ciel rapt, listening.
The water horse
stepping deeper and deeper, withers
glistening, hoof after hoof, tenderly
so as not to frighten
the child. His long
mane she is
holding onto. *And the water horse*
loved the child, I said,
and the child
loved the water horse, and he taught
her to swim. And she swam.

44

.

Listening for the owls who live in the ravine
behind this house. Several? A pair?
I lie awake in the dark of the early year. Call
and response? *I am here. So am I.* The way my children
when they were small would call from their beds,
the way someone might call out to God and wait
for an answer. All these years
and I have not seen them, the owls.
The deer and raccoons climb every day
up the edges of the ravine, through bramble, tangle of
manzanita, madrone. They come to my garden,
eat. And somewhere a horse
lowers himself into water, a child
on his back gripping the coarse dark
hairs of his mane, murmuring *fear fear fear.*

.

Susan tells me she walked
in the hills the day after Odette died,
whom we'd loved, and felt the trees—Monterey Pine,
Eucalyptus—bending over her, witnessing. As though
they could feel it, themselves bowed
with grief. World layered with memory
like leafmulch on the trails, last
year's or the years' before
indistinguishable, turning
to soil, what's under our feet
holding traces of others'
walking, a history
held in wet dark dirt.

Two mourning doves on the deck rail
outside my kitchen window, eating seed
I spread there yesterday. I'm trying to listen
to the radio news and write quickly,
before driving to work.
A reporter is interviewing a man
whose voice is difficult to hear.
How many children do you have? she asks.
He's been deported, she is speaking to him
on a phone that keeps breaking up
in the country he was sent
back to. *Three,* he
is saying. *Three daughters.*
The doves remain, eating. *And how long
since you've seen them?*
They rise, wings making that
muffled sound, into the air. *A long time,* the man
says. *Nearly a year.* The interview isn't
done but it's time
I left the house. He's telling the reporter
the questions the officials asked
at the airport: *What do you keep
in your pockets? Do you own a weapon? What
are your children's names? How many
times a day do you pray?*

.

Hold in this sunlit morning the man
unable to get into the country
unable to see the daughters
waiting for him, wearing
the dresses they put on
only for him. Hold Ciel swimming,
remembering the water horse.
Hold the doves. Hold the named
and the unnamed, the grass, the blossoms
paler now among leaves emerging.

.

How we are saved
and lost. Saved again?
Lost again?

.

Imagine the horse can stride across seas.
Across freeways, stepping
between fast-moving trucks, cars. Easily. Gracefully.
Imagine three children on his back. Daughters.
They are wearing the dresses they've put on
to see their father. Now they are leaving
the edge of the continent; the city
behind them. Their dresses are pink, green,
yellow. The water horse carries them
easily. Clouds and sea birds

pass over them. Now they are under
the waves, they can see
what has always been
impossible to see. They are
in a country that has no
name. Their hair floats behind them
in the water and the horse's mane
floats too and their strong small legs
grip his body and they stay
on his back. The horse breathes
and magically breathes
under the water and they cross
world after world until they can see
a grieving man standing still at the other
end of the ocean, waiting,
it seems, for something
to come to him.

#10

Anywhere

*My friend who trains dogs professionally tells me this on a sunny
afternoon as we walk with our dogs past neighborhood gardens:*

*In the rubble after a disaster, when search dogs are released by
their handlers to find the living and find only corpses, the dogs,
digging out nothing alive, grow weary. Lie with their heads
between their paws, scratch at the dirt, refuse to go back into the
ruins. Become clinically depressed, This is when the handlers send
actors in, who crouch among fallen concrete, plaster, tangled
wires. Lie still, as though injured. As though weak from hunger,
despair. Wait for the dogs to find them, make small moaning
sounds. And the dogs, finding their work not to be in vain, croon
and wiggle, dance, their hind quarters banked against the
wreckage. They bark wildly, joyously, for the human rescuers to
come and lift what has fallen.*

.

At twilight two owls. Somewhere
behind my house, in the ravine tangled
with brush, bramble, debris, construction materials
strewn from the houses uphill, somewhere from two
separate trees they call
to each other, antiphonal.

.

A man drives through the neighborhood
that had been his.
Bombed, buildings razed to the ground,

49

here and there the remains of a car, a television,
bricks of a fireplace. He cannot tell
where he is: predatory birds,
naked corners
where one street intersects with another. Then he sees,
in the distance, the sun at a familiar angle
to a familiar hill. Sun
still there. Hill
still there.

.

There, he says
to the friend riding with him, *there's
where the table was
where I did my work. Every day
at this hour, those shadows of trees
lying across that hill. The window. My hand,
and the way that sunlight fell
on the page I was writing on.*

.

I have waited, uneasy,
for the call of the second owl. Many times
made my way down the ravine,
lingering too long, having to climb back
to the surface in darkness, failing
over and over to see them, wondering
why I was so compelled and who, if
anyone, might be coming to find me.

.

Unseen. Unsayable. In dreams, many
times, a room I did not know
existed: now empty, now filled
with books or shoes. The debris of a life:
mine? Another's? A room never entered.
Let me tell you: I have listened for years
to the longing of one owl for the other, heard
while walking with my dogs
or in bed at night the way
the first question is formed
again and again: *Are you there?* or *Who
is there?* And beneath it, terror. On the other end
of the line, silence. A bird calls and no
bird answers. No hand no milk no mothering God.

.

*And the dogs will not leave until the human rescuers come. My dog
trainer friend tells me they remain even while blasted concrete
keeps showering down, air-space
growing more and more narrow.*

.

Opaque through leaves the late
sun. A man drives
through the ravaged city that had
been his. Knows where he's arrived

only by the angle
of shadows. Everything else
is rebar, bullet-pocked walls. Blown-out
glass of a café. Concrete heaved
against concrete, no space between. Yet
on the slender branches of fruit trees,
white or pink petals.

.

A dog digs frantically among ruins, finds nothing but ruins.
Fallen plaster, tables, papers, shards of ten thousand lives.
Meanwhile the ravaged people march from their homes
carrying children, the old. A few
bags of clothing, whatever they think
might one day again
be of use to them.
Early spring. A light rain
falls, a smell of ozone
mingles with the smell of blood. Acrid.
The dog keeps digging.
Somewhere there may be a breath, a moving hand,
a living eye scanning the darkness.

#11

Berkeley, California
Yemen

A father carries the body of his child
through the streets of a city, past bombs exploding.
He refuses to believe that his child is dead; he
steps over bodies, runs blindly, heedlessly, the child
limp in his arms, toward the hospital:
sees it's also been bombed.
Can you picture this man? Is he one
among millions? Can you see him now,
in front of the smoldering hospital, slabs
of concrete falling, murmuring
Come back to me my treasure, my beloved.
Come back to me. Come back.

.

A child walks out among horses.
She stands among them
in the field, their long necks bent
to eat grass that has grown
tall and sweet again. Months
since her village was bombed,
since she ran from the streets that were burning
onto the field that was also burning. Who
found her, carried her
to where flames could not reach? She remembers
the stars. The half moon. She remembers
being folded into a blanket by hands
she did not know, being fed
coffee and fruit and warm bread.

A refugee camp

The roads were dust. Dust everywhere
and a smell of rot. You found a bird
who had lost its feathers. Children, adults
shat in their cots, screamed until dawn
from nightmares. The bird
hopped around
in the little box you found
for him and you
took care of him and somehow
he stayed alive.
The bombs kept dropping
morning and evening. Sometimes
there were hours of quiet.
People washed clothing.
Smoked cigarettes.
Played cards. Sat together
silently or in conversation. A few trees
had leaves on their branches.
Most were bare.
The bird was small. Not
exceptional. Probably
his feathers had been
gray or brown.
When you took him in your hands
he didn't resist.
He ate. You mixed food
for him, gave him
your own food. Found him insects,
worms. After some time
a faint tuft of down

pushed through his skin as though
he had just hatched, had never known
sky or wind. Had a mother to touch
her beak to his, feed him the way
birds feed birds.

.

I walk out before bed
under the clear sky: Orion,
a bright half moon.
My dog sniffs the air: lemon sage, jasmine
over the neighbor's fence. I have worked, eaten,
spoken with friends. From the ravine
behind my house, an owl calls.
The mice who will be her prey
scurry in blackness
through tangled underbrush.

#12

Berkeley, California

This mortal frame
Basho named the bone house.
Two hundred and seventy bones
when we're born, then
some fuse together
so, grown, we're left
with two hundred and six. (First they fuse; then,
each by each,
crumble.) *Nine orifices*
Basho counts: nostrils, mouth, ears
pee-hole, shit-hole, the eyes?
And for women, one
more. *A hundred bones,* he
wrote, getting it wrong
by half.

.

Brown recluse spider I spent
the night with,
in a cabin
in the San Diego mountains.
I put a glass over her
to trap her, knowing her
from the poster on the wall
of the caretaker's office
for what she was,
able to sicken with her venom.
She lay still
under the glass, now and then
climbing the sides of it, surrendering

56

to the impossibility
of escape as I
to the impossibility of sleep. Full moon
moving across the cabin windows,
an intensity that bound us. Each
studying the other? At sunrise
I woke the caretaker, who
slipped some paper
under the glass, took spider, paper and glass
outside, set her free in dense chaparral.
sharp-smelling creosote. I watched her
disappear, knowing she might go far
or might return.

.

My parents had a child
before I was born
who lived five months
and died one May afternoon
in his high blue
carriage, parked outside the coffee shop
where my mother was having coffee with friends.
He died because the next breath never came.
Until then his breath had been filled
with milk, lilacs, Brooklyn.
I don't remember my mother
having friends; she slept
through the afternoons
as though some punishing
God had condemned her
to loneliness. I didn't even know

the story until I was seventeen
and, looking for something
else, found his death certificate, hidden
from the two born
afterward, all
our childhood shaped
by that dead boy

.

And when the spider was released I experienced
a puzzling mixture of relief and regret, sad
in some way, for the intensity of the night
to be over, though of course I realized
that I too had been released, albeit with no
illusion, in that place of wild grasses,
of safety....

.

Fires circling the cities. Ash in my hair,
on the children's shoulders, their t-shirts,
their sweaters. Are these words, too,
ash? Sky turning ash,
ash falling onto the streets.
How, even
on an ordinary morning
(cars lined in front of the elementary school
down the hill, bright voices
calling across the field),
we are marked. Phyllis, my oldest friend,

holding her week-old grandson, singing him
to sleep. *The world*
is burning she writes me
hours later, *How*
could we have imagined this
when we were children? Tiny mouth
closing and opening around her finger:
Still wondrous, she writes,
in spite of everything.

.

When Ciel had been in the world
five days, I lay
one afternoon on the couch
in my daughter's living room,
my granddaughter's small chest
rising and falling
against my chest while her parents
slept in their bedroom.
Muted autumn light
turning bronze, then sapphire,
then gone. *Lucerito*
de mi alma, I sang to her:
light of my soul.
Fierce glint of solace.

#13

Berkeley, California

I hear it in the deep heart's core.
—Yeats, *The Lake Isle of Innisfree*

Day's last sun pouring over the hills.
Crows in the high branches of Monterey Pine.
My three dogs in the garden,
the oldest among them chasing the youngest.
I have been watching the end of this day
filtered through oak leaves. The book
I had been reading
set aside, plans for work set aside. Beyond
this garden, the city. Beyond that: flood, wildfire.
Yet at this hour
before dusk, this light. These leaves. These dogs.

.

'96, driving across the Mojave, setting out
in the old Toyota
under early stars. Viva's legs
tangled around Nora's in the back
seat, sleeping. Sound of the engine,
thrum of a band (*Nirvana?*) from one of their
headphones tossed on the back seat floor, static on the old
car radio. Otherwise silence. I remember
sitting as straight as I could
at the wheel, willing myself
alert, every cell poised. I remember
being filled, as I drove, with equal parts
of love and vigilance. (Sun
beginning to paint the rocks
vermilion.) Who was I

to have been chosen
to ferry their spirits
across the loneliness of this world?
Bright, wiry animals of their bodies,
chill morning air giving way
to warmth. My daughters, my life. The vastness
stretching ahead of us and behind us. Their breath.

.

Here comes the spirit in its house of bone,
Its rebar. Its walking sticks. Here comes Dashiell,
twenty months, barreling across the room, holding
a stepstool he calls a boat, sailing the kitchen floor,
calling "Pickles! Pickles," knowing the tide
of our love will carry them to him, dill or sour, sliced
thin for his ten fingers to guide them, row them
into his mouth with its seventeen teeth, his belly
with its billions of cells, all the tubes and the linings
of tubes, the ligaments stretching, cartilage grinding, crunching,
the gleaming saliva, synovial fluid, amylase, amytriptolase,
turning pickles to lash, brow, toenail, smile, language.

.

Rosamund telling me years ago
how, emerging into the day
from the long stairs of the Highgate Tube
she felt, suddenly, a joy she had not
known, a lifting (it was during
the war) of despair, of some dark
enveloping cloak. Released. I am thinking now
of the house of bone, of the way, bone
by bone, loss by loss, it's dismantled.

I am thinking of how I picked
blackberries late one August day
after the child died whom I'd carried
six months in my womb. Heat of the afternoon,
hands stained blue with juice, reaching among brambles
for the largest, ripest; and how, walking home
with my basket of fruit, I felt somehow solaced,
lightened. Rosamund dead
fifteen years. Viva, the child I conceived
soon after the other
died, grown. Life that comes to us
over and over: Rosamund
at nearly ninety
in her quiet room
across from the Sangre de Cristos
speaking to me of that moment
years earlier: stepping into the afternoon
of London, people walking in all
directions. Noise. Sky
between buildings. Fragments of conversation.

#14

Berkeley and Richmond, California

My student, weeping, says
there should be mourners
on every street
holding scrolls with names of the murdered:
the homeless, the ill,
the known and the unknown,
the old and the young; the deliberate,
the *tragic accidents.*
A litany of names
as the traffic passes, as rain
falls and falls on the shoulders
of the spared.

.

Signs on the Bay Trail warn of toxic water.
No swimming. No bodily contact.
I leash my dogs, head toward a grassy place
over the hill, wondering
whether oil or chemical, deliberate
or accidental, transient or enduring.
A solitary grebe sails the current.
Morning chill stings my face.
The grebe, her black eyes
fixed on the distance, swims and swims.

.

Always I have been drawn to marshland,
the birds around marshland.
The reeds standing in water,
the salt smell. Tides edging, receding

(Oh beloveds,
I am afraid my life will end
before I speak all the words I have to speak.)

.

Always the leavetaking. Always the words
postponed, forgotten.
Outside, a day unfolding like any other.
I think of the grebe, swimming and swimming.
Dogs racing on a grassy ridge
as the day's sun
rises higher and higher
in a cloudless sky.

.

Emmett Till's mother choosing to keep the casket open.
Erica Garner's mother in the hospital room
where Erica, 27, lies dead after a heart attack,
her father choked to death by police
four years earlier on the street.
Come and see
what we have wrought.
Trayvon Martin's
mother speaking to the crowd, her voice
strong, determined. Come and see children
taught to stand against the walls
of buildings, hands over their heads, and say nothing
while the cop runs his hands
over their bodies.

What is the worth of a life? And what
will you give to save a life? A boy's face,
crushed, beaten, unrecognizable. (*Mourners
on every street,* my
student said...) People—
most of whom had never set eyes
on Emmett when he was alive—
filing in front of the casket.

.

Beside me on the trail I walk
when I leave the toxic water,
an old man limping
on his son's arm, staring up
at jays in the eucalyptus. The son
walking slowly, steadying
his father, shadows
long in the late
afternoon. My dogs
racing each other, doubling back.
Such tenderness between
the younger man
and the old. The undersides
of leaves shimmering in soft
wind, wood sorrel, new grasses
rising abundant from rainsoaked
earth though ruin
be all around us.

#15

Berkeley, California

A scythe moon hangs
among scattered stars
behind the neighbor's roof
as I walk with my dog
in the chill before sunrise. Across the road
a doe and twin fawns
who have been in the neighborhood all summer
graze, leave their tracks
in damp grass. I have feared
for their safety, watched from my window
as the two leap after their mother, she
turning her head. Waiting, not waiting.
September. The mornings darken.

.

I will go home, give my old dog his six medicines.
call Nora to see if Dashiell's cough is better.
Turn on the radio news:
storms sweeping the other side of the country,
another young man shot dead by police.
I speak his name. Look out at the three deer.
Pour seed in the feeders for the wild birds.
The moon is absorbed into the day sky,
shadows of leaves fall across my desk.
The day reveals its contradictions.
Slowly, trustingly, the doe and her fawns
walk back down to the ravine.

.

I knew a boy
whose sister was killed
in a crowded parking lot,
holding her phone, trying to call her brother
to tell him the cops
were chasing her. Someone
thought she'd been shoplifting. She'd run
and the cops came
after her. They claimed her phone
looked to them like a gun. In minutes
she was lying on the cement
between parked SUV's, chest
bleeding, cops emptying the contents
of her bag. Finding nothing stolen.

.

Dadme las luchas
de cada dia
porque ellas
son mi canto: note
from the poet Pablo Neruda
to myself, taped on the wall
over my desk
years ago: curled, yellowing, ink
beginning to fade. And still
I recoil. Renounce. Abandon. Forget.
Martha Hennessy, granddaughter
of Dorothy Day, telling the interviewer
when they are talking of how she,

at 63, may be facing twenty-five years
in prison for protesting the world-annihilating
Trident nuclear
submarine, "My personal life
is irrelevant compared
to the Creation of God
being destroyed."

#16

Berkeley, California

The question being: do I walk past
the man sitting on the corner
of Solano and Colusa
in his wheelchair
in the morning cold?
He is struggling to get money for the shelter.
Dadme las luchas. It's April but
a chilly wind is up.
Cada dia.
I pass him. Sometimes
we speak. Mostly
I walk by, my eyes
turned elsewhere.

.

A woman, eight months
pregnant, is arrested for parking her car
at the wrong meter. Taken to jail, held
there. They sleep in the doorways.
Can't you see, she sobs
to the jailers, I'm going
to have a baby. A couple of years
ago, a woman in a tattered
sleeping bag under
the overpass: she looked
so sick, shivering, eyes sunken, face
pale. We
were walking
to a restaurant

on Lakeshore, it
was late
December. We
stopped, went into
the Walgreen's,
bought her
some Tylenol, a bottle of
water. A box
of crackers.
Eight months
pregnant, alone
in her cell. Came back out, touched
the place on her
sleeping bag where
her feet
were to wake
her since her eyes
were closed. Sorry
I said. (By this
time the friends
we were going to meet
at the restaurant
were texting, wondering
where we were.) She opened
her eyes. Sorry. (What kind
of antiphon am I
writing?) Sorry
again. *This was somewhere*
in the south, in a state
where Black people
get arrested all the time
for nothing: We bought you

(sorry) a few things, I said, you look
pretty sick, maybe this
will help you a
little. *A car*
parked at the wrong meter, a broken
tail light. Can we get you
anything else? Do you need
to go to a hospital? Lights
from the passing
cars. *God, please*
just let
my baby be
ok. A small rain
beginning to
fall. Smiling
weakly up at
us, lips
parched from fever.

.

My students this morning talking
about how we are all complicit. Complicit
in the death of the infant
in detention, complicit
in Trayvon's death, Kalief's death, the death
of the woman holding her phone
in the parking lot, the death
of the skeletal child in Yemen on the cover
of the magazine I have kept on my desk
for months now, promising myself
I will not forget, I cannot forget.

71

.

As though remembering were itself
a penance or a kind of balm.
You ask if it soothes
and I tell you it does not. Maybe nothing
does. I am thinking now of the late afternoon,
maybe a year ago,
when I drove past the phone store,
heading for someplace else,
and saw two cops roughing up
the homeless autistic man
I've seen sitting
on the outside window ledge
of that store for years. Day after day. Speaking
to no one, occasionally drinking coffee
the baristas at the coffee shop
give him for free. I stopped my car,
pulled into a parking space, yelled at the cops
to leave him alone. *I know this man,* I
said, approaching. *He doesn't bother
anyone. He just sits here, watching.
They know him at the coffee shop.*
The older cop took his hands off the man,
the younger one didn't. The older one
stared at me. *What do you know about him?*
he asked. *He doesn't bother anyone,* I
repeated, turned to the man, asked him
*Is this ok with you? I mean, that I'm trying
to stop them from hassling you?* No words. A slight nod.

Staring into the crowded street, not looking
at me, at the cops, at anything. A bus
passing, cars, kids eating ice cream. The younger cop
still with a hand on the man's
shoulder, asking me now, *What do you*
want us to do with him, lady? There has been
a complaint. People complain
about him sitting here. What do you want
us to do? Louder now, his thick hand
tightening on the man's
bony shoulder, *Do* you
want to take him home?

#17

Berkeley, California
Yemen

I speak the name
of the Yemeni child, Amal, who, this
morning, I read, died
finally of starvation.
Seven years old. No more
hunger. No more
pain. Amal.
I sit at my desk
on this quiet street, the neighbor's
gardener clipping the jasmine,
mild late afternoon air
saturated with fragrance
of hyacinth, narcissus. Amal.
Amal. Amal. The sound of a rake raking
leaves drenched by yesterday's rain.
A day like any day. Amal's mother
rising from where she has tried to sleep,
looking across the room at a blanket:
shapeless, covering nothing.

.

There should be mourners
*on every street…*When
I was a child we played
telephone: two paper cups and a string
stretched the length of the hallway, my friend
and I each behind a closed
door, listening for
the other. *Here I am. Where*

are you? (Owls
in the ravine behind
this house.) Practicing
losing and finding. Rehearsing.
Losing and finding and losing
again. The hallway
empty of everything but our
game of
longing: *Can you*
hear can
you hear
me hear
you?

.

This is how a child of seven
dies of starvation: *(I need*
you to not
stop listening) When no food
is taken into the body,
the brain depletes sugars,
then protein. Muscles grow
small. Useless. The organs
too start shrinking: liver
heart kidneys. *(Once*
she played
in the street with
other children) The body
loses its defenses. Most people
who starve die ultimately
of some *(Ran)*

infection that penetrates bodies
without defenses. *(Maybe rode*
a pink plastic
scooter like the girl
I saw yesterday speed
down the hill across
the road from where
I was walking with my
grandson) Amal's
body without
defenses. Amal's mother
without defenses. Her country
without defenses. If not infection,
then the heart *(don't*
turn away now, don't say
this is too dark
to hear; think
of the little vessels
tightening, narrowing; think
of the healthy
child speeding down
the hill yesterday
afternoon in northern
California on her
scooter, hair
flying, arms
bare in her yellow
sundress though
it was windy, about to rain)
ultimately
stops beating.

It takes
energy for a muscle
to push blood
from one chamber
to another. Chambers empty
of blood (rooms empty
of a child's
footstep) empty of
sound *(Amal*
Amal) empty of

.

Daily the Creation of God
destroyed. In front of the phone store
on Solano Avenue
a homeless spark of the Creation of God
sits, too exhausted to stand, bags
in his lap. Dylan, my fifteen year old corgi,
limps down the stairs, hind legs
that have served him (Creation
of God) to swim lakes in the Sierra, race
circles around the garden,
still carrying him, though each hour
more spent. I tend him, give him
his medicines, gently wash the white fur
on his belly (*O world I cannot
hold you close enough:* young
Edna Millay…)

.

for Amanda, Justin and Mabel

The city analyzes soil from your garden,
tells you it's safe. Lead, arsenic
levels ok. Now
you can plant vegetables you'll eat
through summer. Now you know
the leaves of chard, leaves of kale,
won't infuse you with poison
in their turgid greenness.
This is the care you take
for the child
you conceive:
that what you offer
is greenness, carefulness. Clouds
racing in from over the Bay,
the garden bright, then
shaded, then bright again. You bend
to put the small seedlings
into the ground, stems so thin
it hardly seems they'll stand
in this wind. Yet they do. Tenderly
you pour a slow circle of water
around each one, your dog
tossing his toy
across the garden. Catching it.
When, I think,
has the world not been
a windswept contaminated
place into which

to bear new life? *(Young leaves*
soft and rounded will
redden, lengthen...) And should that
be the measure?

.

(Oppen choosing, after one
book, to renounce poetry: the need
of the world too great, the hungry
too hungry. Who is it
who could think
poetry is enough
to feed the children? Organizing
in Brooklyn, enlisting
to fight fascism though
he's more than old enough
to sit out the war, choosing exile
under McCarthy.
Twenty-five years
later, dreams, in Mexico,
of a rusting truck
parked in a field—

.

A girl in a detention camp
holds a younger child's hand.
She has spent the morning
combing his knotted hair
with her fingers. Hot
sun, concrete
reflecting it hotter.

He sits patiently
on her lap, not making a sound.
She picks out the lice.
He is not her brother.
Whoever called him
by a name
has been sent
somewhere else. The girl
talks to him, doesn't know
if he understands,
gives him the name
of a child she played with
once, somewhere else.
The boy doesn't
look up, stares
into the yard. Her hands
remembering now some
tenderness (where? from
whom?), touching his scalp.
Louse by louse,
crushing them hard
between her small fingers.

.

—and slowly, slowly
begins again
to write poems.)

#18

Leningrad, Russia
Berkeley, California

Then I learned how faces fall apart
How fear looks out from under the eyelids
How deep are the hieroglyphics
Cut by suffering on people's cheeks

—Anna Akhmatova, *Requiem*

Akhmatova standing in the visitors' line
at the Leningrad prison. 1935.
Other lines in the cities for bread, milk.
No heat in the houses, mothers
leaving their children
at orphanages so they can be fed.
Silence or weeping as they wait
A woman near her (not
knowing Akhmatova
was a poet?) whispers, "Can you describe this?"
And "Yes," the poet answers her. "Yes."
And something like the shadow of a smile
crossed what had once been her face.

.

The Amazon burning.
Trees that speak
to each other underground,
warn of disease, invasive
insects; trees,
that share 70% of our DNA. Do we
too, *forked*
animals, standing on line

in the Leningrad winter,
packed (forked branches
barren of
leaves) so tight in detention cages
that we can't (cloaked
in ice, consumed
by flame) lie down; do
we too speak
more authentically not
with our words but with
our cells?

.

A man walks in the Sonoran desert, finds
a pile of torn rags, picks them up,
understands they were the last
clothes someone wore
while crossing the border,
someone whose body
was eaten by animals, birds
of prey. Not a bone, not even
a hair: All
that remains
are these faded scraps
of the clothes they wore.
He returns
the next day
with a wooden cross
he has made. At the point
where the boards intersect,
he nails

a small disc, painted
with an image the color
of the sun-bleached rags.

.

Most of the clothing,
is found
under trees, because people
sit down in the shade,
then find they can walk
no farther…
All that exists of them
is the place they died.
Cross after cross in the sand
This was a child. This
might have been
an old woman. Nine hundred
crosses. Not a single name.

.

The fourth blossom on the sprig of scarlet freesia
breaks open sometime this afternoon
in the clear glass vase on my kitchen table.
Someone I'd never seen before
gave it to me from her garden
when I passed and said
how startling their color was,
as two people whose last name
I've never known, whose paths for years
have crossed mine

in the early morning,
walking my dogs, left on my front steps
some stalks of asparagus they grew,
their names scrawled in pencil on the paper bag,
Fred and Beth,
of whom I know nothing
but their stride, the hours they keep.

#19

Berkeley, Callifornia
France
Germany

Odette told the story
of the poet on the truck
on the road to the gas chambers.
Passengers sitting in silence, some
reciting prayers to themselves
others reciting the names
of their children, their parents.
Looking out at the stark landscape, sky
mottled with clouds, dirt
the tires stirred up. The poet,
who had been in the Resistance,
took the hand of the man
beside him. Held it, began—
as though this were happening
somewhere else—
reading the man's palm.
You will have three children,
he told him, *a house*
you will build yourself,
apricot trees in the garden.
He turned, took the hand of a woman.
You will have grandchildren, he
said. *One will be a violinist*
and play Bach partitas
for you when you're old.
The truck continued its solemn journey.
Barbed wire. A wind coming up from the north.
The driver driving. Eyes straight ahead.
Hands stretching toward the poet:
Read me. Read me. Read me.

.

The driver of the truck, certainly
an agent of the state, so moved
by what he was hearing,
turned the truck around.

.

Which is not to say that some of those
who had been there
may not have been taken, even
the next day, back
to the death chambers. And the poet himself
dead months after the liberation
from typhus contracted in the camp.

.

Odette, who had been a hidden Jewish child
in a village in France where she'd had
to change her name, learn
to cross herself, say
the *Notre Père* —where
for months she didn't know
if her parents were dead or alive—
told the story to Susan, who
told it to me. Tell me: is there a grief
you would spare yourself?

#20

Berkeley, California

Jasmine climbs
over the slatted fence, fragrance
carried this mild afternoon
through the bright air. This too
mi canto: for the boy
slain on the sidewalk
a few miles from here
where he went to buy milk
for his family's
breakfast.
For his mother
who sent him out
on that errand.
Sirens. *Las luchas
de cada dia* must yet
be accompanied
by joy, the way
when I stayed at the refugee camp
we sat on the narrow, crowded terrace
and ate *mujaddara:* lentils and rice,
sumac, roasted onions.
We sang and we laughed as night
overtook us, as the helicopters
of the Occupation
kept circling, circling.

.

A man I knew who was a firefighter
rescued a family from a burning apartment—
two kids, a mother, a grandmother—
and carried their dog down the ladder
last, a big dog, Pit mix: heavy, muscular.

He could feel the dog's skin burning
as he stepped down, the dog crying, the kids
crying too on the sidewalk across the street.
He set the dog down, wrapped him
in a blanket to stop the fire
eating the flesh. A smell
of singed fur, the dog writhing
on the ground
but alive. I knew the man
because he brought the dog to the vet
one day I was there
and told me the story.

.

All of us inextricably
intertwined, a hall
of mirrors
mirroring mirrors, no way
to tell where the first face begins.

.

After the fire the family
moved somewhere else,
couldn't keep the dog,
couldn't afford
his vet care;
so the firefighter,
who had already paid for the dog
to be treated, took him
home, kept him,

lay with the dog (whose fur
would never grow back in the burned
places, whose skin
was puckered, discolored)
in bed at night
dreaming sometimes
of what it was to step
backward down that ladder, flames
all around them, fear in the grip
of his gloves so intense
he could feel it, a kind of love
beginning there
that made the scarred animal
holy to him, and beautiful.

Coda

for M.

London
Calabria

A braccio a braccio we walked
up Muswell Hill Road.
September, 1973, speaking Montale's
lines, *Cio' che non siamo, cio'*
che non vogliamo. We too, knowing
what we were not, what
we did not want. Our lives, our friendship
tethered to poetry. Hours reading Dante
aloud, Petrarca, Leopardi; walking
under the broadleaved trees,
buses passing, arms locked.
Then that afternoon, stopping
to buy bread in the corner shop,
the headline: Allende murdered in Chile.
Singers whose songs we had sung together
in the narrow front room of your house
arrested, brutalized. Victor Jara's fingers cut off
in the stadium
before they shot him, fingers
that played the strings of the guitar.

.

Some survived on chestnuts during the war,
bread made from chestnut flour, steamed chestnuts
for breakfast. Ten men killed
in the *piazza* for every *fascista* felled. Children
dragged from their houses—six, seven years old—
to witness the fascists' firing squads:

everyone from the *paese*
forced to witness. *A braccio a braccio* we walked
all that first year I lived in London,
and the years that followed.
You in your black skirt,
red sweater, waiting for me at the window.

.

Gracias a la vida we sang,
Violeta Parra, our act of resistance,
walking toward Highgate Wood
in the rain. I sing it now, Mariolina, after
forty-seven years of friendship
across a continent and an ocean,
across our children's births, their
growing. Our grandchildren.
Years of visiting you in your garden, walking
the Heath, speaking of poetry
and the broken world, trading books,
songs. Now a cancer
divides and divides in your body.
Like another friend I dreamed of, you say
you need nothing. The garden behind your kitchen
is enough, you tell me, even
in autumn. Voices
of friends. *Gracias. Gracias*
Violeta, *Gracias* Montale
and Ungaretti, *gracias*
to the sky through high branches, the dogs
racing down paths through
the Wood, generations
of dogs. *Gracias* to the telephone, the rain,

91

the smell of old books, the commas
and semicolons, the Italian vowels.
Gracias to *cammomila* at three in the morning
after hours of talk, *gracias* to *Bella Ciao,*
to anoraks, to the pact we made
that we would endure. *Gracias*
that we know the end is coming
and for this time
that is still ours. *Gracias*
to the *partigiani,* to Diorissimo,
to texting, to the sea
in Siracusa where we floated for hours,
gracias to mild night air after scorching afternoons,
to the blue mop mopping the dark red tiles
in the corridor.

.

All love is a rehearsal for death,
Cardenal wrote after the death
of his friend Thomas Merton.
And so, *amica mia,* we rehearse.
When George died
two days after Viva was born
and I sat on my bed,
nursing her, watching her lips
move while she slept
in the shapes of sucking,
Mary called from the hospital
where George had been
struggling for days
to let me know it was over,

and told me, *Now maybe*
we can start
to remember the good things.
Cardenal, whose tender elegy for Merton
we read together,
dead himself now,
and Eavan Boland
who named
the *merciless inventory*
of love, whatever it is
that brings us (these late
November days, gingko and sumac
turning, incredible violet
light at afternoon's
end) to the edge of
the tolerable, holds
us back.

2016-2020

Notes

#1   Nothing you do will make a difference
yet it remains essential that you do it

Attributed to Gandhi

#4   Starfish Wasting Disease. According to John Platt, in *Treehugger* (January 31, 2019), this disease, first noted in the summer of 2012. is attributed to warmer water temperatures due to climate change.

#5   Rexroth is the poet Kenneth Rexroth. The poem I cite is *Kings River Canyon.*

> *My sorrow is so wide*
> *I cannot see across it;*
> *And so deep I shall never*
> *Reach the bottom of it....*

The other poets mentioned here are George Oppen, Denise Levertov, Muriel Rukeyser, Adrienne Rich, and Allen Ginsberg. All were influences on my work,
all are deceased.

#8   Kalief Browder was imprisoned on Rikers Island in 2010 at age 16 for allegedly stealing a backpack. He remained imprisoned for three years, awaiting trial, with nearly two spent in solitary confinement. He was released when no evidence against him was found and died by suicide (hanging) two years after his release. It is understood that his suicide was a result of mental and physical abuse sustained in prison. He was 22 when he died.

The camp I mention was a camp on the island of Badia, in the Adriatic, for children orphaned by the NATO wars in Bosnia/Serbia (the former Yugoslavia). My daughter Viva and I worked there in the summer of 2001.

#9   The Susan I mention is my dear friend Susan Griffin, author of *Women and Nature, A Chorus of Stones,* and many other books. Odette was Odette Meyers, another dear friend, whose book *Doors to Madame Marie* documented her experience as a hidden child during the Nazi Occupation of France.

#12   The song I mention singing to Ciel is a Sephardic song, origin unknown to me. Montserrat Figueras sings a version of it on her CD *Ninna Nanna.*

#15   The lines from Pablo Neruda (who did **not** write them to me directly!) are from his poem *El Hombre Invisible* and translate as follows:

> *Give me the struggles of each day*
> *Because they are my song*

The lines leading up to these read as follows:

> *Dadme para mi vida*
> *todas las vidas,*
> *dadme todo el dolor*
> *de todo el mundo,*
> *yo voy a transformarlo*
> *en esperanza.*
> *Dadme*
> *todas las alegrías,*

aun las más secretas,
porque si así no fuera,
cómo van a saberse?
Yo tengo que contarlas,
dadme
las luchas
de cada día
porque ellas son mi canto,
y así andaremos juntos,
codo a codo,
todos los hombres.

Martha Hennessey is the granddaughter of Dorothy Day, co-founder of The Catholic Worker. In April of 2018 Hennessey and six others broke into the Trident Nuclear facility at Kings Bay, Georgia, and were arrested for "conspiracy, destruction of property, and depredation of government property." The nuclear warheads in the Trident Submarine could destroy the world many times over. At the time of the writing of this section Hennessey was facing twenty-five years in prison for that action. In November, 2020, she was sentenced to serve ten months. The quote is from an interview with Amy Goodman on *Democracy Now!,* November 25, 2019.

#16   Trayvon Martin was murdered at sixteen while walking home from a convenience store in Florida on February 26, 2012. Kalief Browder appears in poem #8 of this sequence.

#17   Edna Millay (Edna St Vincent Millay) wrote the poem *God's World,* whose first line is
Oh world, I cannot hold thee close enough,

published in 1917. She was the first poet whose work I took as an influence on mine, in 1961, at age fourteen.

#18   Anna Akhmatova, one of Russia's greatest poets, was born in Odessa, The Ukraine, in 1889. The passage and incident I cite here are from *Instead of a Preface* to her great poem *Requiem,* also an influence on my work. I quote it here:

During the frightening years of the Yezhov terror, I spent seventeen months waiting in prison queues in Leningrad. One day, somehow, someone 'picked me out.' On that occasion there was a woman standing behind me, her lips blue with cold, who, of course, had never in her life   heard my name. Jolted out of the torpor characteristic of all of us, she said into my ear (everyone whispered there). Could one ever describe this?' and I answered, 'I can.' It was then that something like a smile slid across what had previously been just a face.

Tucson-based sculptor, Colombia native Alvaro Enciso has installed over 900 crosses in the Sonoran Desert to   honor immigrants who have died there. His project is named *Where Dreams Die.* He spoke of this project on *Democracy Now!* on August 21, 2019.

#19   Odette and Susan appear in #9 of this sequence. The poet in this amazing and true story is Robert Desnos, French surrealist poet who joined the Resistance and was captured. Susan records this story in her essay *To Love the Marigold.* I have embellished but not changed the important truths of it.

#20   The poets mentioned here are the Nicaraguan Ernesto Cardenal; Thomas Merton; George Oppen; Mary Oppen and Eavan Boland. From 1973 until their deaths, the Oppens were very close and inspiring friends to me.

Coda   This is dedicated to a beloved friend, a poet and translator with whom I first discovered Italian poetry during the time I lived in London in my twenties.

About the Author

Anita Barrows was born in Brooklyn, New York, in 1947 and has lived in the San Francisco Bay Area since 1966. Among her awards in poetry have been grants from the National Endowment for the Arts, the Ragdale Foundation, the Centrum Foundation and the Dorland Mountain Arts Colony, and publications by The Quarterly Review of Literature and the Riverstone Press. Her three poetry chapbooks from The Quelquefois Press in Berkeley are housed, among other places, in the University of California Library (Berkeley and Santa Cruz), the British Museum, and libraries in Baghdad and Kabul. She has had two previous books published by The Aldrich Press (Kelsay Books). Anita Barrows and Joanna Macy have collaborated on four translations of the work of Rainer Maria Rilke, including *Letters to a Young Poet,* and Barrows' novel *The Language of Birds* will be published by She Writes Press in 2022. She has also done translations since 1972 of novels, poetry, plays and non-fiction from French and Italian. Barrows holds a PhD in psychology and is Institute Professor of Psychology at the Wright Institute, Berkeley. She maintains a private clinical practice in Berkeley and is a mother and grandmother and companion to a household of dogs, cats, and birds.

Made in the USA
Middletown, DE
02 July 2021